mei mei *little sister*

mei mei *little sister*

PORTRAITS FROM A CHINESE ORPHANAGE

by Richard Bowen

Introduction by Amy Tan   *Afterword by* Karin Evans

CHRONICLE BOOKS
SAN FRANCISCO

Library of Congress Cataloging-in-Publication Data available.

ISBN 0-8118-4734-9

Manufactured in Singapore.

Design by Vivien Sung

Distributed in Canada by Raincoast Books

9050 Shaughnessy Street

Vancouver, BC V6P 6E5

10 9 8 7 6 5 4 3

Chronicle Books LLC

85 Second Street

San Francisco, California 94105

www.chroniclebooks.com

This book is dedicated to the fates and their two most joyful expressions in my life, *Maya Elizabeth Meiying Bowen* and *Anya Cybele Xinmei Bowen* and to the care they deeply feel for their little sisters.

So through the eyes love attains the heart:
For the eyes are the scouts of the heart.
—Guiraut de Borneilh (ca. 1138–1200)

THE UNFINISHED STORY OF OUR LIVES

by Amy Tan

I often think of the intersections in our lives, those that are planned, those that occur by chance. Some encounters we hope for, particularly love, and, alas, some meetings never happen despite what we wish. I think of how those intersections have the potential to change us, our character, our circumstances, our hopes. I think about how they add to the unfinished story of our lives.

The photographs in this book are for me one of those intersections. In fact, within days of seeing just a few of the photos for this project for Half the Sky, the changes began. Old friends from out of town dropped in to visit and brought with them their newly adopted daughter from China. The following day, I left for China, and a friend, a volunteer with Half the Sky, arranged for me to visit an orphanage in Chengdu. There I played with babies, talking to them in my own babyish Mandarin while silently wondering about the events that had brought these girls there, and those that had led me there as well. When I left the orphanage, I continued with my life and those babies continued with theirs. But now I wondered what would become of them.

For the next few weeks, everywhere I went in China and the United States I saw Chinese baby girls in new strollers pushed by their besotted Western parents. It was not merely coincidence, of course. Once we become aware of a particular thing that touches our heart, we notice it over and over again. It's a matter of focus and paying attention to the details in the world.

Richard Bowen paid attention to the details. A cinematographer-turned-photographer for this project, and the father of two adopted Chinese daughters, he visited a number of orphanages in China, both those with Half the Sky sponsorship and those that had not yet begun. He took photos of girls, both in the summer months and in the wintertime, as you can see by both the beachwear and the sausagelike jackets. With few exceptions, he chose girls who were beyond babyhood, and thus the ones likely to have already missed the window for adoption. He did not intentionally pick the prettiest or the sickliest, the happiest or the saddest. He did not tell the girls to smile and look at the camera. He did not pose them, except perhaps to place some of them on a chair or a stool. The background is a neutral seamless, so that the girls' essential selves might better stand out, unfiltered for the moment by where they live. After taking many thousands of photos, Bowen chose these hundred for the book. It was a difficult selection process, and in explaining his choices to me he quoted the late photographer Richard Avedon's famous axiom: "Each picture is accurate. No picture tells the truth."

And so we see only this particular intersection, this moment in these girls' lives. The girl in bridal wear (page 56), she has the cool detachment of an ingenue on a magazine cover. The pensive girl with both hands on her knees (page 63), is she thinking of the mother who recently gave her up or wondering if she will still be in time for a snack? The sturdy girl in a sundress with one leg crossed over the other (page 133), she has the expectant look of one waiting for the show to begin. And what about the pretty girl with two beribboned buns a few pages earlier (page 127), the one with the small furrow in her brow? What is she worried about? Why do so many of the girls in these photographs have a similar pensive knot? Is it merely because of the *waiguoren* in front of them? Or is the bunched-up brow a regular feature? If we waited another moment, would the children be showing us gap-toothed grins, as does the beribboned girl one photo earlier (page 126)?

I continue to examine each girl's face intently. I laugh at seeing the Chinese version of American careers expressed in childhood: a princess, a petticoated cowboy, an Indian chief (page 65). I also admire the trio of costumed kids earlier in the book (page 49), who look like typical trick-or-treaters, looking up at the person who has just answered the door but having forgotten their lines. As I take in the one hundred faces—shy smiles, laughing cheeks, and turned-down mouths—I try to intuit the feelings behind each. This one who's staring seems so serious, uncertain, even scared, or maybe she is simply shy. And what a look that one girl has!—so saucy, the little prankster who easily wins people's hearts. Surely she'll find her way in the world.

But what about this dull-eyed girl, and this one here and that one there? A few of them seem passive and detached, without protest or wariness, curiosity or demands. I sense that for them this moment is neither better nor worse than what came before or what will follow. Many of the babies I saw in the orphanage had this same passive look, despite a cheery environment and loving caregivers. And I've come to think that this is the look of a little girl who has never known that her face is the most beloved of anyone else's in the entire world, that her teary needs matter more than anything else, that she has a never-ending supply of hugs she can claim at any time for warmth, or consolation, or bliss. Oh, but they are still so lucky to be in such good orphanages! I say this to comfort myself.

And now I am conscious that I am looking at these girls not just through Bowen's lens, but from my own perspective. I must be careful not to fall into either helpless pity or the romanticism that I can rescue them all. I must avoid the ethnocentric gaze of comparing these girls to luckier or unluckier ones. I want to see each girl for who she is. It's impossible, of course. But it's good to ask every now and then: What is the essence of any of us beyond the comparative assessment of others?

I also wonder what the purpose of our looking at such photographs is. These are girls we will likely never meet, whose stories will remain for us forever incomplete, mysteries if we choose to think about them. It seems at times too painful to look at these abandoned girls if we cannot directly take them into our arms and make their lives instantly better.

Yet I think it is important to look. As with any photograph one might see in a history book or a family album of snapshots, they are portals to another's consciousness in a particular time and place. For as long as we look, we can imagine. With a bit of imagination, we can inhabit that moment over and over again, that mind and heart, that smile or frown, those desires and needs. We can look and hope to know more. That is the start of compassion, I think. The rest just naturally follows. And before we've even finished turning the page, those girls are already part of our lives.

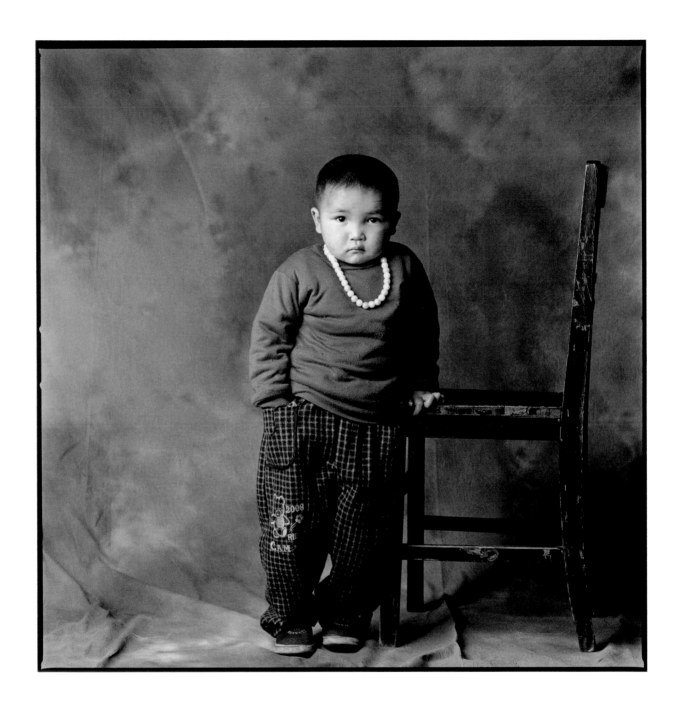

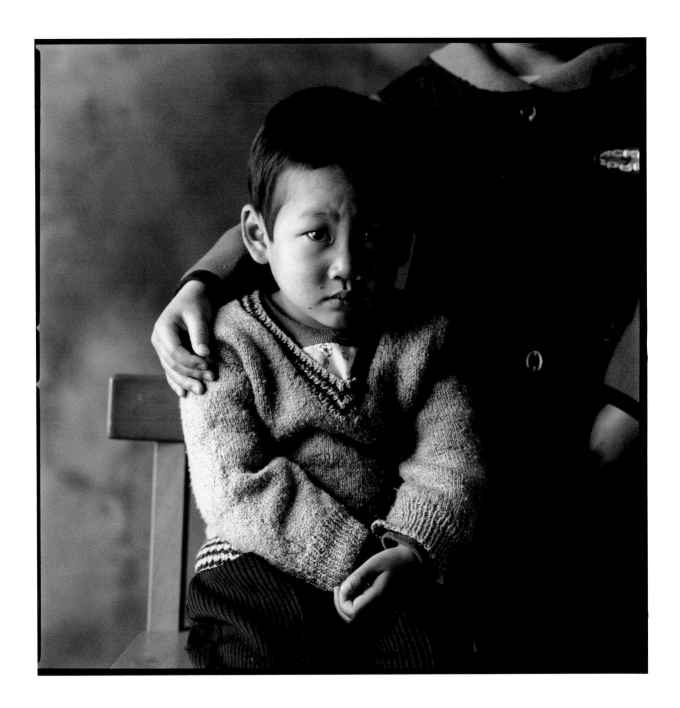

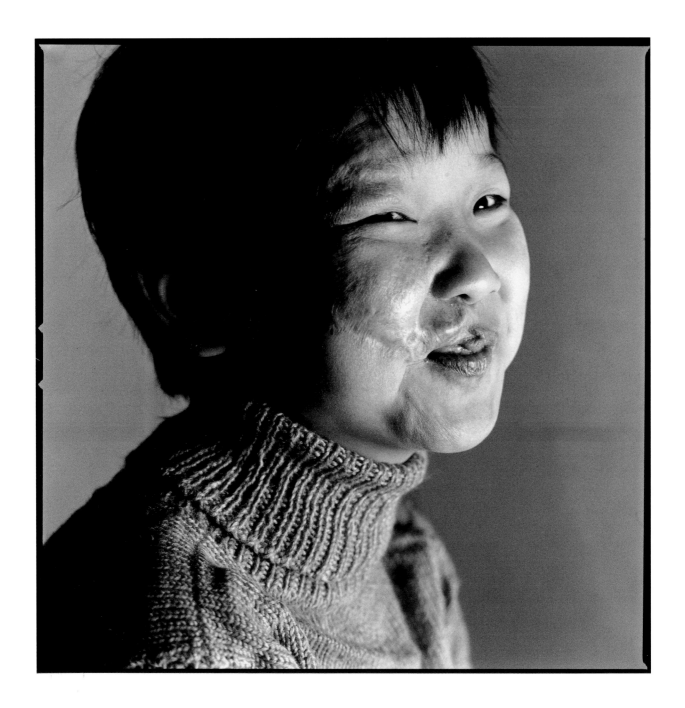

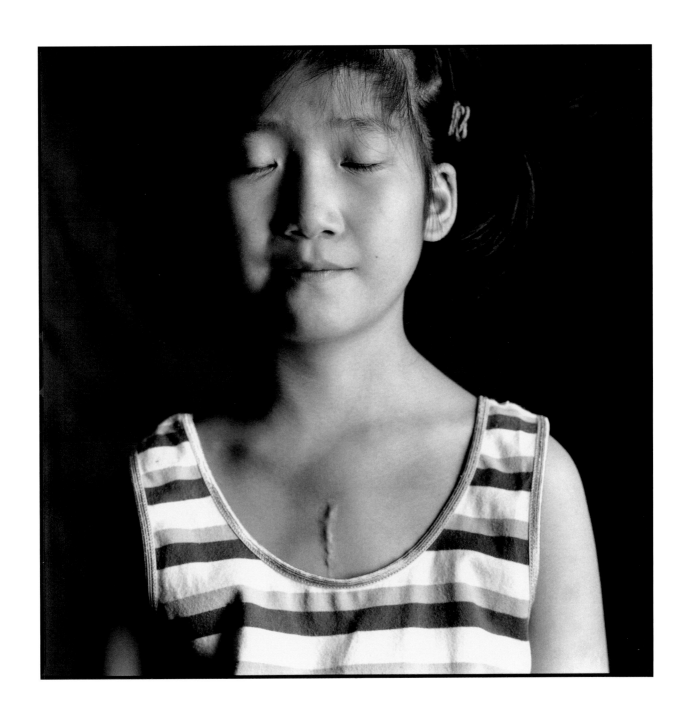

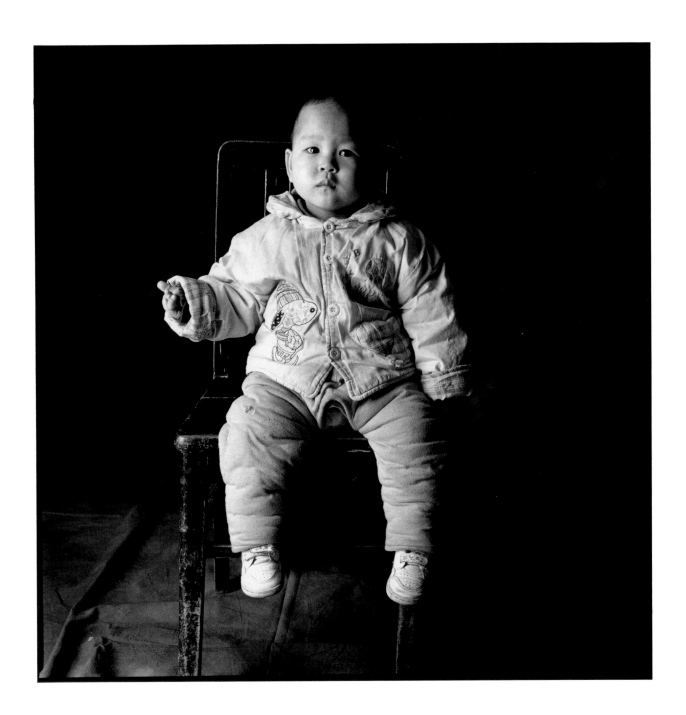

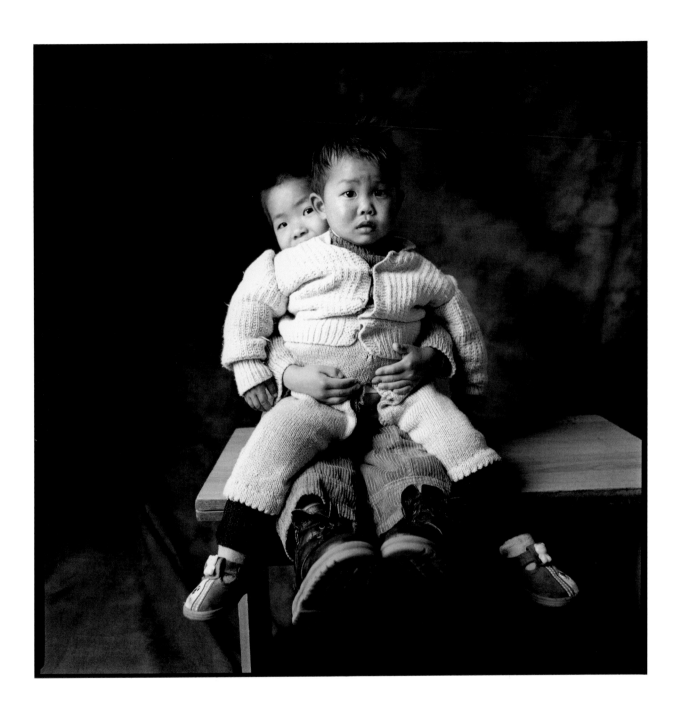

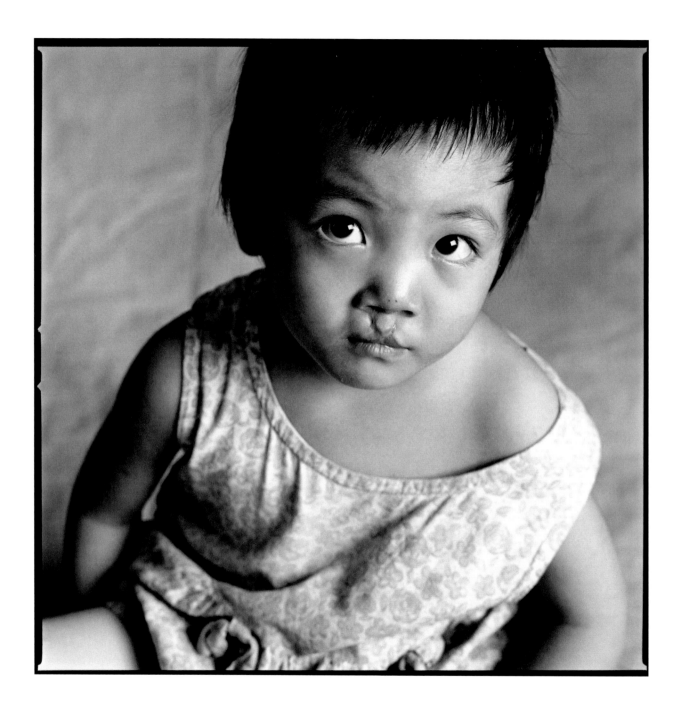

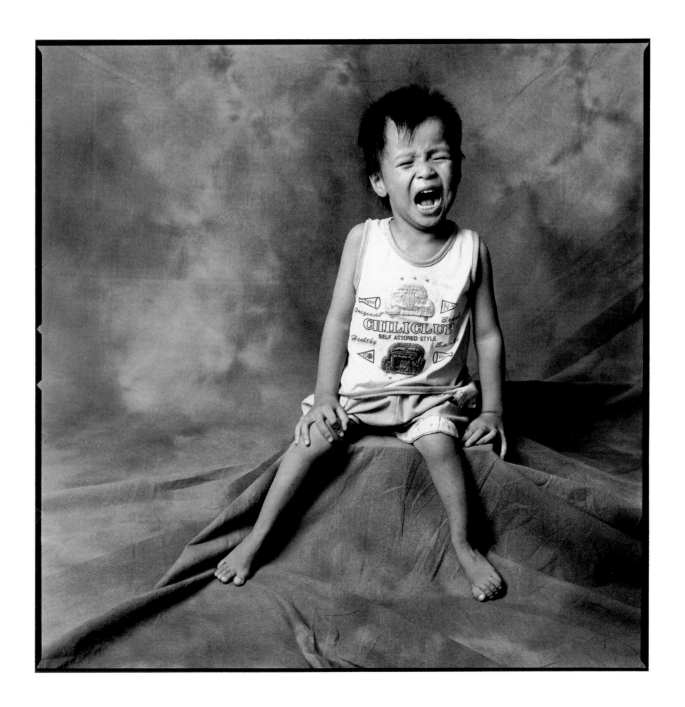

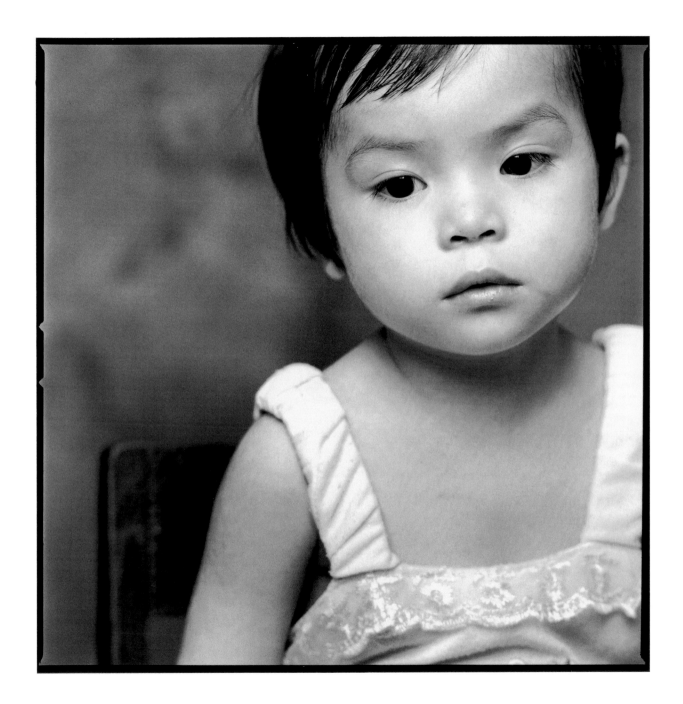

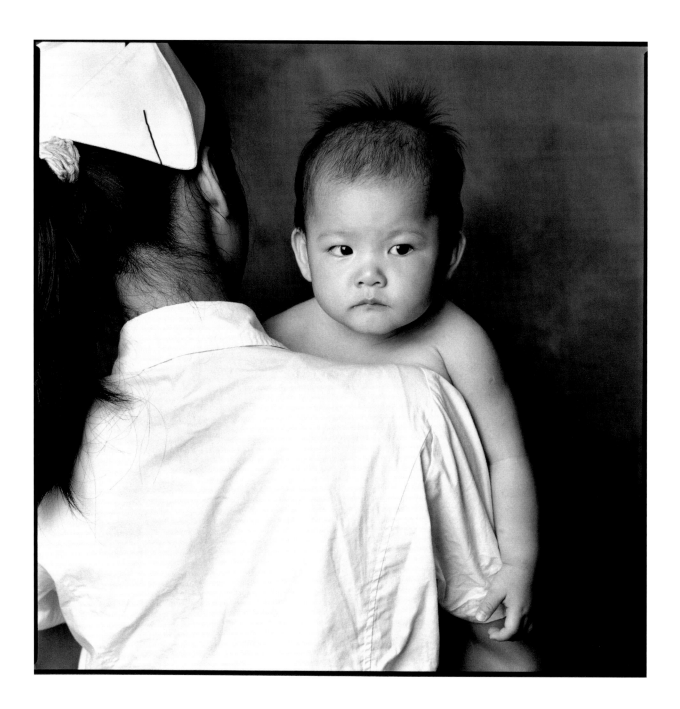

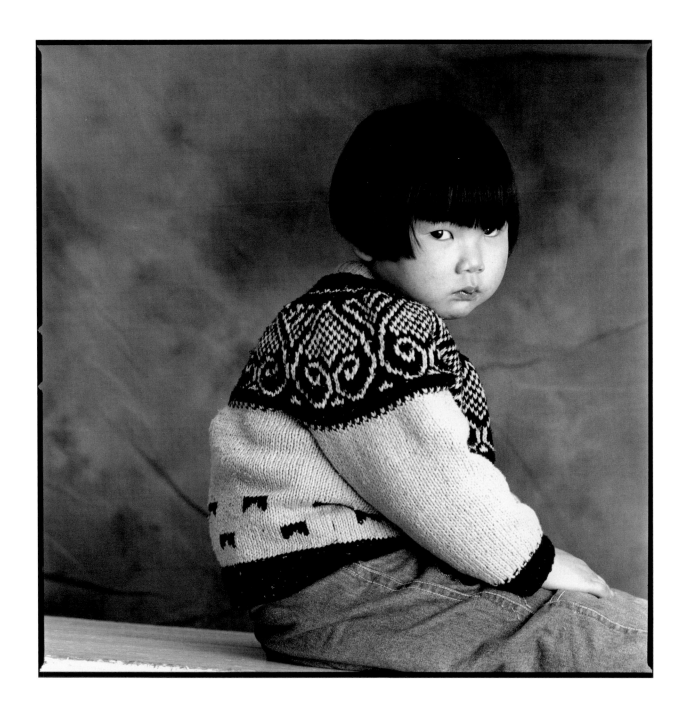

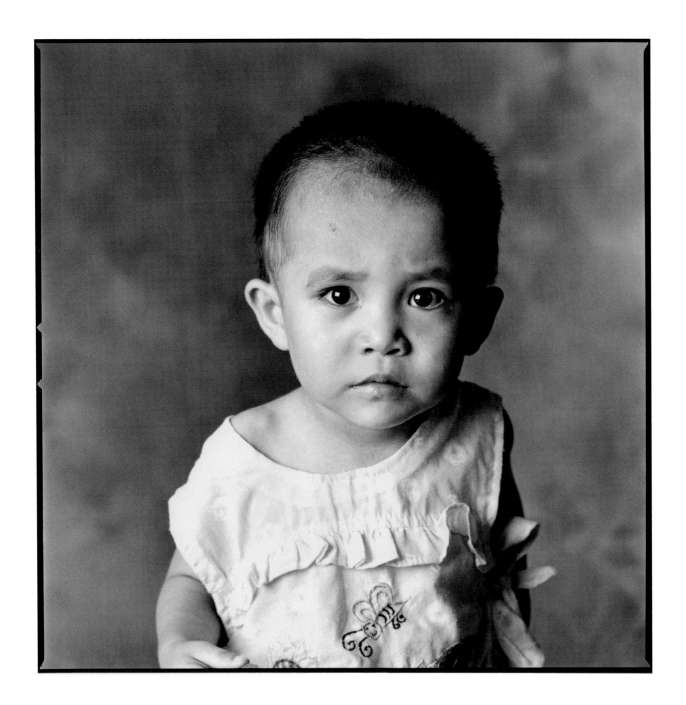

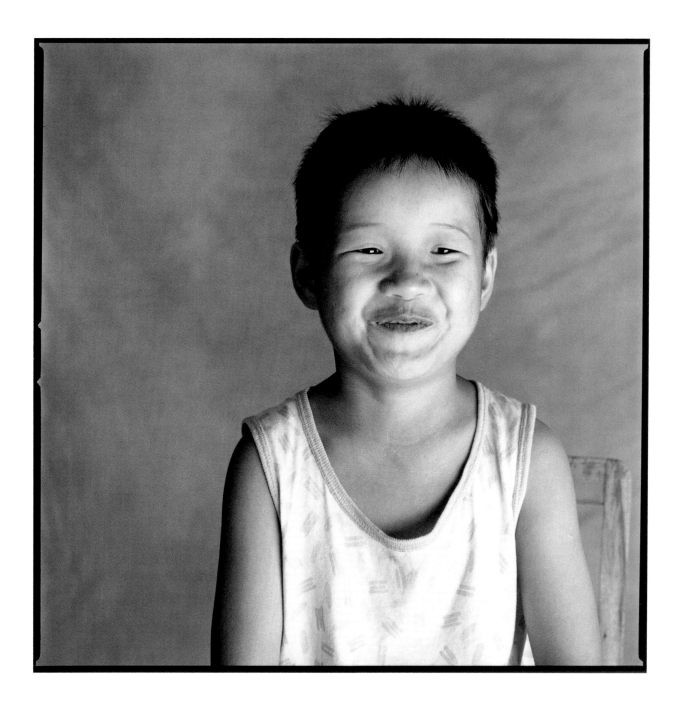

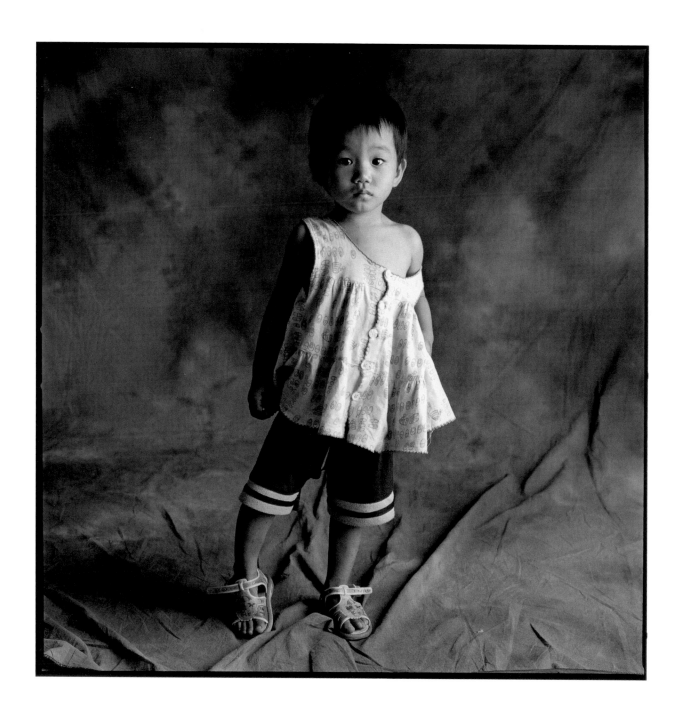

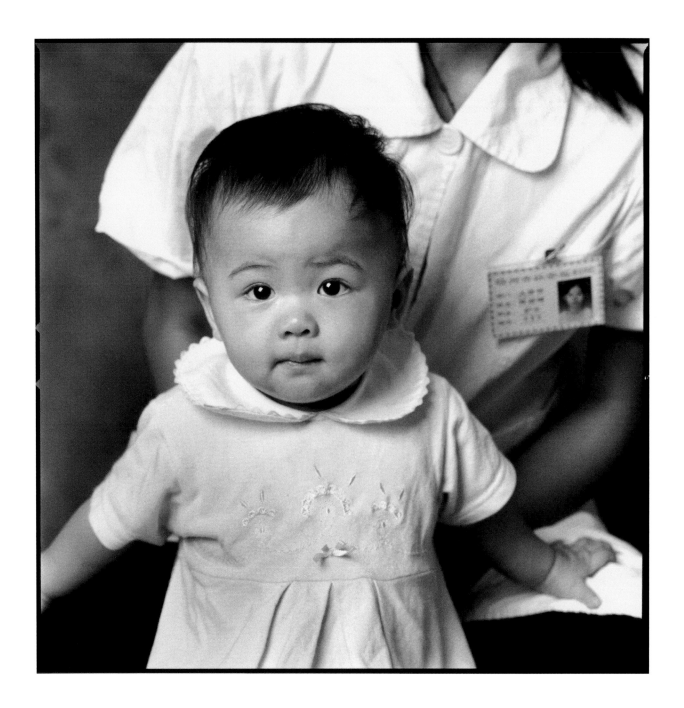

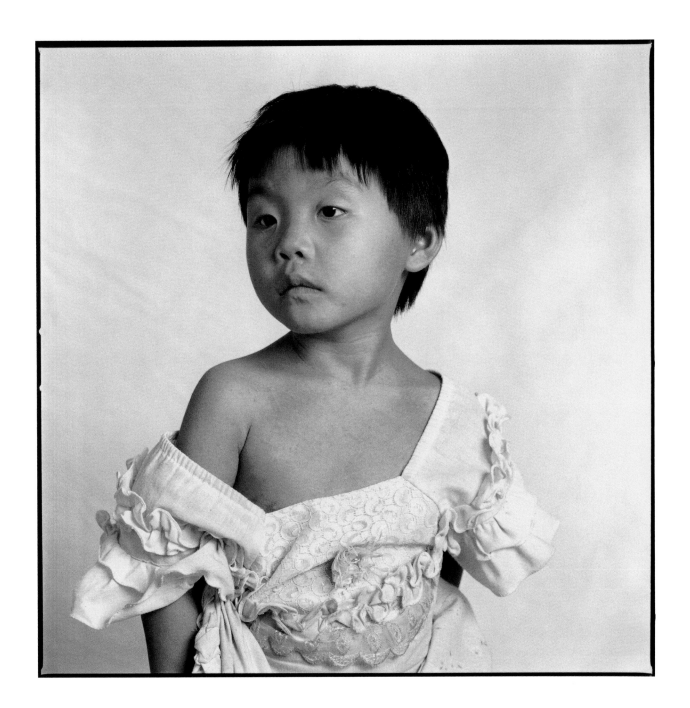

126

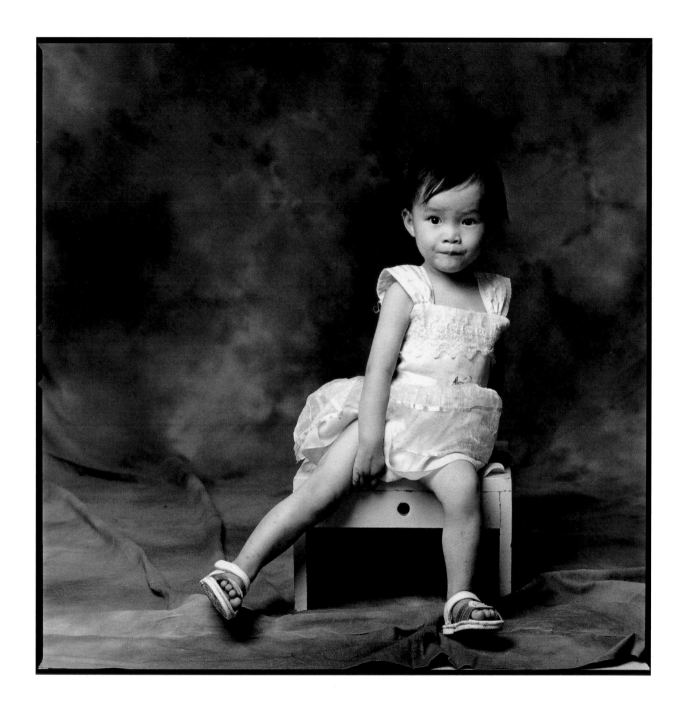

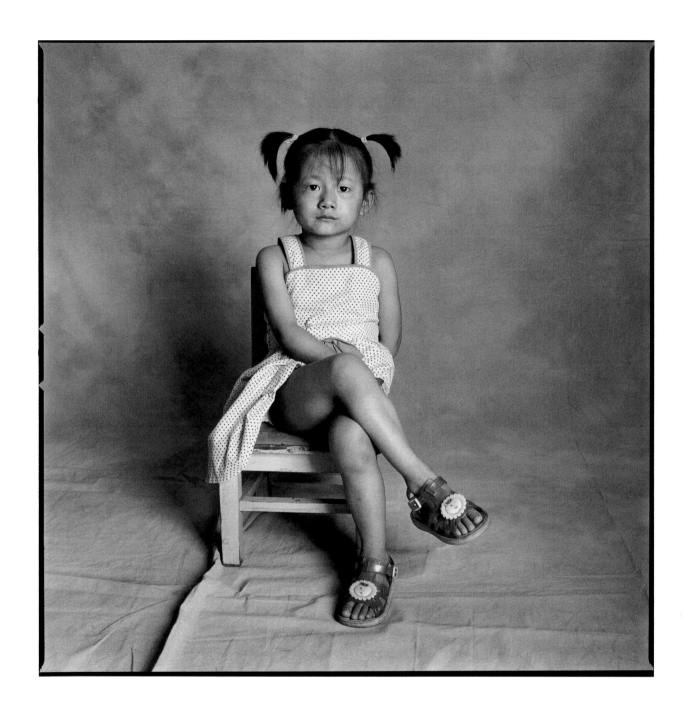

AFTERWORD

by Karin Evans

As I look into the eyes of the children in this book, I see them from a mother's perspective. I feel the presence of my own daughters, who spent part of their early years in Chinese orphanages. The girls who remain in these institutions may be a world away, but for families like mine who are blessed with adopted children from China, they are as close as our hearts. Were it not for a twist of fate, any of our daughters might still be there.

In the cities of China, tucked somewhere off the beaten path, are the buildings that house the local social welfare institutions, and inside, the small faces, the children left behind in the shadow of progress. Walk through an orphanage, and you'll be forever changed. Newborns, newly found. Toddlers in their wheelie chairs. Older children who have been in the institution for years and will be there years more. Little ones with cleft palates, burns, and other scars, visible and invisible. Totally undeserving of the world's hardship, they represent each of us at our smallest and most vulnerable. The human family is meant to fill such immense primal loneliness. A mother's embrace is needed, a father's hug, a grandparent's indulgent smile. Yet these children have lost everyone at once.

It's impossible even to know how many there are. I look at the photographs showing all the babies in their cribs (on page 144) and know that this cluster of children can be multiplied by thousands, tens of thousands. Each day, more arrive on the doorsteps of the institutions, swept there by the forces of random misfortune and contemporary pressures. A line of ancient Chinese poetry reads, "To be an orphan . . . how bitter is this lot"—an old lament that aptly fits a modern condition.

When China's stringent birth control policy went into effect in the 1980s, limiting most families to a single child, the orphanages began to fill, overwhelmingly, with girls. Though the picture is a complex one, a basic cause was the combination of the strict enforcement of this policy and the age-old Chinese family system with its traditional preference for sons.

There are other explanations: poverty, medical needs a family has no hope of meeting, natural disasters, and individual tragedies. Picture a young rural woman toiling six or seven long days a week for a pittance at a big-city plastics factory, living in a dormitory with other workers—no family nearby, no safety net, no way to care for a child.

Whether these children were found at a few days old wrapped in a blanket on a busy bridge, or discovered at four or five, wandering alone with a few belongings near a police station, they now live in state-run institutions and await uncertain futures. The local authorities post their pictures, but no one comes forward. They stand before the camera bearing the world's sorrow, poverty, and hardship on their small shoulders. Ghosts hover around them—the parents, grandparents, siblings, aunties, and uncles who've left no traces.

Once in the institution, as many as ten thousand of the children, usually the younger ones, are adopted each year by Chinese families, and thousands more by families from abroad. But the vast majority of these girls remain in the orphanages. As they grow older, their chances of finding a family diminish. And so they wait. When they are old enough to leave the institution, they will go into the world by themselves, with no one to count on.

Their faces haunt me. The girls gazing into the camera are braver than children should have to be. And yet their spirits peek through—a shy smile, an impish grin, a sturdy stance. What a difference a little encouragement could make.

New arrival, March 2003

New arrival, January 2002

That sense of hope is what has drawn me and others to Half the Sky Foundation and its work. It's a way to give something to the children left behind—a nanny, a nursery, a schoolroom, a teacher. With the help of thousands of families who've adopted children from China, the good people of the China Population Welfare Foundation and the China Social Work Association, and countless volunteers and supporters, we join hands and go to work, training teachers, painting bookshelves, hiring nannies to hug the little ones. And before long there is laughter in the nursery, excitement in the classroom, art hung all over the walls. The older girls are even given some individual help before they enter the outside world.

These children, though they don't know it, are responsible for creating an extraordinary bridge, a coming together of family and friends from East and West, engaged in a common effort—to help China's orphaned girls come out of the shadows. It's just a start and not nearly enough. We all know that. But once you've looked into their eyes, it's hard to turn away.

Finding place, Guangzhou

Finding place, Yixing

Finding place, Chuzhou

HALF THE SKY FOUNDATION

No one knows the numbers. Each year thousands, perhaps many hundreds of thousands of China's children lose the love of a family.

Some of those who survive are sent to state-run welfare institutions near the place they were found. There they live with fifty to five hundred other homeless children; 95 percent of the healthy ones are little girls.

Orphanage workers, often untrained and overwhelmed, do their best to provide the children basic care. It is all they can do. That is why Half the Sky Foundation was created.

Named for the Chinese adage "Women hold up half the sky," Half the Sky provides loving nurture for infants, enrichment and early intervention for preschoolers, and personalized learning opportunities and guidance for older children.

The organization, created by families who have had the good fortune to be able to bring Chinese children into their lives, works to help each child grow up feeling that she is someone. That she has a voice. That she is seen and heard. That she matters and that she is loved.

Here are a few of the almost three thousand children whose lives Half the Sky touches daily. They are our family, our children's *mei mei,* little sisters. Ours is a family with open arms. We welcome you to join us.

Jenny Bowen, Executive Director
www.halfthesky.org

Half the Sky
Foundation
半边天基金会

LITTLE SISTER'S NAMES

All the girls who appear in this book reside within China's social welfare system, which cares responsibly and well for their physical needs. Nearly all the girls pictured will spend their childhoods in an orphanage; a lucky few have been, or will be, adopted in China or abroad. At the time of photography, all the girls were either actively attending, or about to begin attending, Half the Sky programs. Their names, listed here in English and Mandarin, were given by orphanage staff and are listed randomly to protect their privacy.

Village billboard, "These are new times. Girls are as good as boys."

元双 Double Vitality	彩缤 Vivid Profusion	衡兰 Everlasting Orchid	何英 Brilliant Wisdom
秋庆 Autumn Celebration	文舞 Exquisite Implication	丽传 Beautiful Legend	进群 Progressive Gathering
梦燕 Dreaming Swallow	敏明 Agile Intuition	丽蕾 Budding Beauty	小毛 The Little One
晓茹 Little Endurance	子娟 Graceful Posture	迎雯 Welcoming Cloud	棕瑶 Palm Sonnet
婕 Feminine Ingenuity	培琼 Nurturing Beauty	广英 Extensive Wisdom	建晴 Constructive Clarity
盈 Abundance	敏俊 Handsome Agility	佩岚 Admire Haze	仁芳 Benevolent Fragrance
新蓉 Graceful New Beginning	过玲 Passing Exquisiteness	芳静 Tranquil Fragrance	晓雨 Morning Rain
文柳 Gentle Willow	晓叶 Morning Leaf	容钰 Tolerant Precious Jade	贞吉 Faithful Prosperity
备 Ready	如霞 Peaceful Morning Glow	圣珊 Sage Coral	维维 Safekeeping
春妮 Adoring Spring	丰 Prosperous	冬兰 Winter Orchid	君玲 Refined Chastity
秋莲 Autumn Lotus	冬雨 Winter Rain	英芬 Fragrant Heroine	北晴 Sunny North
夏虹 Summer Rainbow	诚洁 Pure Honesty	蛟靓 Magnificent Dragon	唐盼 Hopeful Expectation
新秀 Rejuvenated Beauty	康洋 Brimming Security	乐冰 Joyful Integrity	博雯 Erudite Colorful Cloud
和香 Peaceful Fragrance	冬顺 Gratifying Winter	忠婉 Loyal Gracefulness	银翠 Silver Emerald
元屏 Protected Vitality	乐洋 Copious Joy	英茹 Enduring Flower	诺 Promise
春香 Spring Fragrance	博文 Erudite Scholar	佳露 Wonder Dew	信 Faith
丽章 Literary Elegance	微号 Intricate Appeal	丁美 Little Charming	琦芳 Fragrant Jade
秋书 Harvest Tale	乐乐 Happy Joy	站凯 Standing Victory	和平 Peaceful & Calm
文梓 Flourishing Rhetoric	紫玉 Lavender Jade	脂莹 Plentiful Rouge	永僖 Everlasting Happiness
千桓 One Thousand Dignity	雨甜 Sweet Rain	童薇 Innocent Rose	元缘 Predestined Beginning
春田 Idyllic Spring	新远 Pristine Journey	丁月 Lilac Moon	永炫 Everlasting Dazzle
资玉 Nurture Jade	元元 New Vitality	岚桂 Misty Laurel	永诺 Everlasting Promises
仁海 Merciful Sea	田田 Plentiful Harvest	脂淑 Virtuous Rouge	元慈 Vitality Kindness
庆华 Magnificent Celebration	欢美 Charming Jubilee	桃仪 Abundant Dignity	明珠 Glowing Pearl
晓艾 Beautiful Morning	沙丽 Delightful Sand	放美 Blossom Beauty	超 Exceed
夏全 Summer Flourish	寒梅 Enduring Plum Blossom	筷晨 Dawning Bamboo	
诗 Poetic	文慧 Literary Intelligence	和玲 Harmony Bell	

BIOGRAPHIES

Owen Roizman

Richard Bowen and his wife Jenny adopted the first of their two Chinese daughters, Maya (*Meiying*, Beautiful Hero), in 1997. A year later, he became a founding member of the board of directors of Half the Sky Foundation. Soon after adopting their second daughter, Anya (*Xinmei,* Joyful Plum Blossom), in 2000, Richard began photographing the children in this book, eventually traveling to China four times and setting up his camera in fifteen orphanages . . . "to document these girls and let them speak to the world."

Since 1981, Richard has worked as Director of Photography on a dozen feature films and hundreds of television commercials. He has also produced two feature films and directed numerous commercials. He is an active member in the American Society of Cinematographers and belongs to the Academy of Motion Picture Arts and Sciences. He and his family share two homes, in Berkeley, California, and Beijing, PRC. Though he has always been an avid still photographer, *Mei Mei* is his first photo book. His royalties from this book are being donated to Half the Sky Foundation.

Amy Tan is an internationally acclaimed author of many books including *The Opposite of Fate: A Book of Musings, The Hundred Secret Senses, The Bonesetter's Daughter, The Kitchen God's Wife,* and *The Joy Luck Club.* She has also written several children's books, including *Sagwa, the Chinese Siamese Cat,* which Amy helped turn into a popular animated cartoon series for PBS. On one of her many trips to China, she had the opportunity to tour an orphanage and see first-hand the effect Half the Sky has had in improving the lives of the girls who live there.

Jenny Bowen is the executive director of Half the Sky Foundation, an international organization with over 20,000 supporters that provides services to 3,000 children in China. A former screenwriter and award-winning independent filmmaker, she founded Half the Sky in 1998 along with her husband Richard and a small group of adoptive parents. She represents Half the Sky on the advisory board of the Chinese Government's National Committee for Orphans and Disabled Children.

Karin Evans is a journalist and the author of *The Lost Daughters of China: Abandoned Girls, Their Journey to America, and The Search for a Missing Past* (Penguin Putnam). The mother of two little girls from China—Kelly and Franny—she serves on the board of directors for Half the Sky Foundation. In 2003, she was selected as one of five "Women Who've Made a Difference in the World" by the International Museum of Women.

ACKNOWLEDGMENTS

This book might not have happened, and certainly not in its present form, were it not for the generous guidance, help and encouragement of the following: *Linda Austin; Aaron Bowen; Jenny Bowen; Tamara Cervantes; Kate Chase; Steve Cohen; Jessica Deng; Karin Evans; Ron Fricke; Ken Hausman; Jim Manera; Anchee Min; Adam Moore; Barbara Moulton; Owen Roizman; Amy Tan; Yang Lei; Yang Shuo; Ivy Yu; Vivian Wong Zaloom; Zhang Zhirong; Amy Treadwell, Vivien Sung,* and all the good people at Chronicle Books.

And the countless, nameless caregivers working in China's welfare institutions.

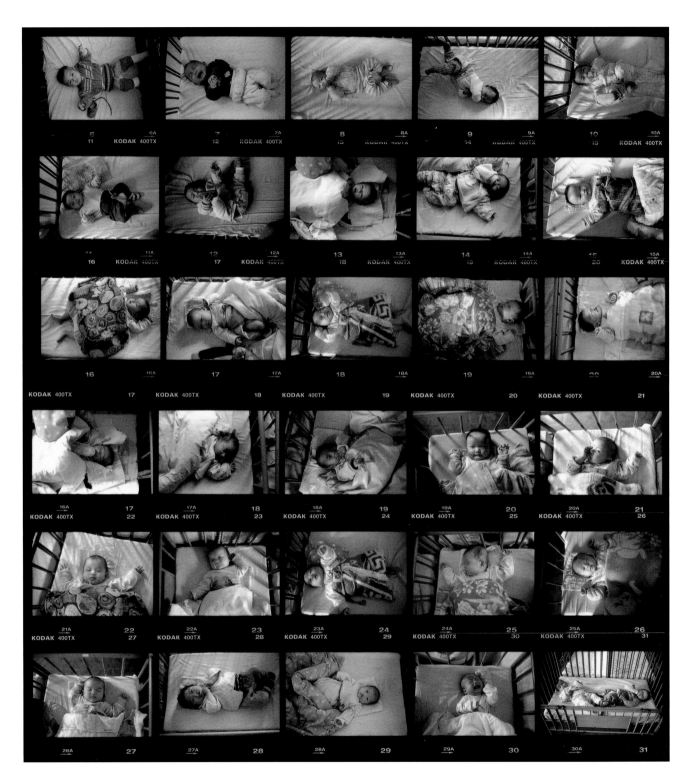